SOCIAL MEDIA INTENSIVE

Using Social Media the Right Way

Tammy Moorehead, H.C.

Tammy Moorehead, H.C.
Visit my website at www.thecantonmarketplace.com

Printed in the United States of America

First Printing: August 2019

CONTENTS

Social Media Intensive is meant to be a basic guide for home-based, small business owners, looking for information on how to use social media to benefit their business. The information contained in this book is not meant to be the end all plan for your marketing strategies but is intended to raise your awareness and help you make informed decisions about your personal business.

As an entrepreneur for the past 25+ years, I have taken expensive training seminars, read hundreds of books, and tested many theories on my own businesses, and have come out the other end wiser (at least I think so, LOL). I believe that every business and every entrepreneur must create a marketing plan that is unique to them and their business. That is the approach of this book. Throughout this book, you will be given information you can use in your business. We will explore a variety of methods for marketing your business via social media. You will be given specific examples that have been shown to work, but ultimately, it will be up to you on what you implement into your business. My purpose is to give you the tools to make smart marketing decisions!

— TAMMY MOOREHEAD, H.C.

I personally would like to thank and dedicate this book to the more than 400 vendors and small business owners that I work with every day. What started, as a way to, help our local community, has grown into a family of caring businesspeople, looking to better themselves, their community and lift up each other! I am truly blessed to have so many great people standing with me and allowing me to do what I love every day – helping others! Thank you

SOCIAL MEDIA'S PLACE IN YOUR BUSINESS

Do you really need social media?

Using social media will help your business skyrocket!

S OCIAL media. Just those two words alone will cause differing opinions on how it should be used for business today. In fact, there are hundreds of businesses that conduct trainings on the "right way" to use social media to make your business skyrocket. Really? While some of the basic concepts of social media marketing will work for everyone, the fact remains that every single business and business owner needs to market their business differently. Why?

Let's start with the basics – as a home-based business, do you, honestly, consider yourself a small business? If you answered no, then you need to take a hard look at what you are doing. It is more than just a hobby; you are trying to build something for you and your family. Something that you hope one day will make you enough money to relieve some pressure, allow you to get out of debt, give you the freedom to vacation. Whatever your desires for your business, it is in fact, a business.

Now that we are all on the same page, it is important to understand that your business is unique and different from everyone else. Even if you have the same product, you are the difference between my business, your business, and your competitor's business. YOU!!!! When you realize that you are the difference maker in your business and stop trying to "do" what the other gal (or guy) is doing, you will suddenly find the keys to your success. This concept is something that many will disagree with, but I have seen it all too often. Once you make an action plan for your social media marketing that fits you and your business style, you will suddenly see a difference in the number of followers you gain, the number of sales you make, and how your business is all of a sudden the talk of the town!

Why use Social Media in your business?

Whether you are the type of person that has embraced social media and all its glory, or one of those people that have tried to keep it at bay, the fact remains that social media has become the new way to market your business effectively and at the most reasonable price.

Gone are the days where you could put an ad in the paper and sell everything in a weekend, or just attend a few craft shows and sell out your table. Today, word-of-mouth has become the most popular way to sell any product or service, and in today's technological world, social media has become the most popular platform for word-of-mouth!

What does this mean for you and your small business? You MUST embrace social media if you want your business to succeed. But more than just embrace it, you will need to learn how to use it to your advantage, how to adjust, how to recognize the need for change, etc.

It is not about spending hours in front of your computer, or on every social media platform, it is about learning what each platform is capable of producing, determining if that will benefit your business, and then putting a plan into action.

So, no matter what type of home-based, small business you have, social media is a necessity to grow your business and meet your goals!

Where to start!

The very first thing you need to do in using social media for your business, is learn everything you can about social media – how to use it, which platform to use, when to use it, and most importantly, how not to turn shoppers away!

The number one mistake I see small businesses doing on social media is posting their business dealings on their personal social media platforms! Number 2 most often mistake I see is posting the same thing over and over, and to multiple groups/pages!

STOP!!!!!!

If you are having trouble getting interaction, sales, new followers, etc., it is most likely because you have either been blocked by people, or you are posting the same thing, day after day, week after week. Posting the same thing and expecting a different result is never going to work!

To really understand social media and how to use it effectively for your business, you first need to know social media etiquette – the important do's and don'ts of social media.

Social Media 101 – Etiquette

It is important for you to realize that posting on social media is not a guarantee you will gain followers or get sales. You have to put in the work, and most importantly, you need to follow proper etiquette on all platforms.

The first thing you need to realize is that your personal twitter account, personal Instagram account, and personal Facebook account are just that – Personal. Keep the things you post on them related to your personal life. Sure, it is ok to post something related to your business occasionally, but if you are putting post after post about your sale, joining, etc., chances are you have already been blocked by lots of people.

If you do not have a business account set up for each of the platforms you will use in your marketing, the first thing you need to do is set them up! (Remember, you are running a business, so treat it like a business with it's own pages).

The second thing you need to realize about social media marketing is that sometimes less is more. Creating a post and then sharing it to multiple pages and groups is only hurting you. You need to realize that people belong to many different groups and follow lots of different pages. Sharing a post to multiple pages and groups gives the appearance to those in multiple groups/pages of desperation. That is the last thing you want your shoppers to think. Stop sharing your posts in multiple places. Instead, your goal is to get the followers in those other groups to follow your page and join your groups (we will discuss this more later).

Lastly, you need to understand that throwing money around to try and get followers is just that – a waste of money. There are ways to get organic traffic to your social media platforms without spending hundreds of dollars, but you have to be patient. Contrary to popular belief, it does not happen overnight. Good organic traffic, organic followers, organic shoppers will stay with you if you treat them right. It is organic traffic you want – those are the ones that are genuinely interested in what you have to show/offer them.

Now that you understand the basic etiquette of social media and you stop doing all those things that are hurting you, let's dive into what you should be doing for your   business!

DETERMINING THE RIGHT SOCIAL MEDIA OUTLET

Attraction Marketing

Choosing the right social media platform will affect your attraction marketing

A TTRACTION marketing. You have probably heard the saying many times, but do you really understand what attraction marketing is? While there are many different variations of what attraction marketing means to you and your business, the bottom line is you need to understand it and use it to grow your business.

Every single thing you do to market your business, draw in customers, build your brand, is attraction marketing. Using social media is just a tool you use to help further build your business, draw in customers, and build your brand. Every flyer you pass out, every post on social media, how you set up your booth at a craft show, and yes, even how you respond to other posts, can all affect your attraction marketing.

So, when you are deciding which social media platforms you want to use in your marketing plan, you must keep attraction marketing in mind. Each social media platform you choose to use in your marketing will play a specific part in attracting customers and building your brand.

Goals you want to accomplish

Before deciding which social media channels/platforms you will use in your marketing plan, it is important to understand your end goal. What do you want to accomplish? Gain followers. Get sales. Recruit others. Earn a trip. Advancement in your company. The list goes on and on. What you want to accomplish will directly determine how you market and what social media platform you will use.

Your first assignment – sit down over the next 7 days and make a list of the goals you want to achieve in your business. Think seriously about what you want. Put the list in a place where you can read it often, make changes, add to it, etc. At the end of the 7 days, take your list and create a "final" goal list that you can hang everywhere! Put as a screen saver on your computer and phone! Type and put on the refrigerator. You get the idea. Make sure your goals are front and center, daily, and that everyone knows what you are working towards.

Now that you have your goal list, we can discuss the different social media channels/platforms. Once you understand each platform, you can then decide, based on your goals, which will work best for you!

Facebook

Facebook is the most widely used social media channel today with more than 2.4 billion users, and extremely popular with small business marketing. There is really no other platform where you can reach such a vast number of people!

Facebook can help you get your message out to a large number of people, quickly; however, you do need to exercise some caution in how you market your business on Facebook.

As we already discussed, the best attraction marketing using Facebook involves having a business FB page. Your business FB page is the face of your company. Make sure you take the time to set up your page correctly and completely! (detailed information on this is covered later in this book)

Your business FB page will allow you to create groups, where you can offer specials and communicate information to specific groups, create events, create a shop, do live videos to demonstrate your product, and post information about your business and products whenever needed.

One of the best features of Facebook, it allows you to market to specific people. You can choose a specific radius to concentrate on, choose people based on the zip code they live in, their hobbies and interests, etc.

In my opinion and experience, every small business owner must have a business FB page and use it consistently to achieve their goals.

Twitter

Once widely popular, Twitter has dwindled over the last few years. With just under 70 million users, Twitter can help you build brand awareness. Twitter is really best suited for those small business owners that have a website and/or blog. It can help drive traffic to your website and blog through captivating snippets.

Because users on Twitter re-tweet often, you can increase your followers quickly by posting tweets that are interesting. Content creation is key when using Twitter!

In my opinion and experience, small businesses that are looking to educate and get information out to people, should be using Twitter in conjunction with a website/blog.

Instagram

Instagram is increasing in popularity because it is visually appealing to many. Now with over 1 billion users, many small businesses are starting to use Instagram to help build their brand and promote their business.

The main reason Instagram is becoming more popular, is because people today are more visually driven than in the past. Photos attract attention. A great photo will not only get you a follower on Instagram, but put some great content with it, and you will get interaction. Interaction on Instagram tends to be a little easier than on Facebook, therefore, many businesses are jumping over to Instagram.

In my opinion and experience, Instagram is a great addition to any marketing plan, if your product and business has lots of different images it can use and share. Since it is a visual platform, if you do not have at least 1 different image to use daily, do not bother. However, if you have a different image you can post daily on Instagram, then it is a great addition to your Facebook marketing – and nice little side note.... When you set up your business FB page, you can set up your business Instagram page at the same time and hook them together!

<u>Summary</u>

While there are lots of different social media channels/platforms you can use, the 3 listed here have shown to provide more attraction marketing bang for your buck, than the others. The only other social media channel worth mentioning is YouTube. If your business model is about doing instructional videos, then you should consider adding YouTube to your social media lineup.

PLAN OF ACTION

Becoming the Master of Your

Business Marketing

Analyze your goals to create your action plan.

N OW that you understand the importance of social media marketing for your business, and understand the difference between the most popular channels/platforms, it is now time to make a plan of action. To execute any marketing strategy, you must have a plan.

As we briefly discussed in the last chapter, you need to understand what goals you want to accomplish – what is the end result? If you took the time to do the goal exercise, you will already have a list of the things you are looking to accomplish with your marketing. If you did not do that exercise, go back and do that now!

Now that you have your list of goals, let's get started in creating a plan of action. The purpose of having this plan, is so that you can execute, analyze, adjust, and become the master of your business marketing.

Note - For the purposes of demonstration, I will use the goal of obtaining more followers throughout the rest of the book.

Step 1 – Analyzing Your List

The first thing you need to do in creating your action plan is to analyze your list of goals. Go down through your list and beside each goal, make a note of what is needed to help you reach that goal.

For example, if I had increase number of customers listed on my goals list, then I would write beside it – increase followers, create business FB page, create business Instagram page, create customer group, interact daily.

Go through your goal list and write down everything you feel you need to do to reach that goal. (If you feel you are stuck on this step, this is where enlisting the help of a business coach or doing a small group session with others can help you).

Step 2 – Create Your Task List

Now that you have analyzed your goal list, make a final list of actionable tasks you need to accomplish. Write down this list and put in order of the tasks that are listed most.

For example, from my list above, I would write down each task I have listed, in the order of the ones most often used. If I had increase followers beside every goal on my list, then I would list – Increase Followers – first on my task list.

Step 3 – Create your Social Media Outlet List

Now that you have a list of tasks that need to be completed, you can take that action list and place beside each item, which social medial platform will help you achieve the end result.

For example, to increase followers, I would write Facebook, Twitter, and Instagram beside that task, because all social media platforms will help you increase followers.

Step 4 – Create your Action List

This final step in creating your action plan is the most intensive step. Now with all the information you have written beside each goal on your list, create your action plan to accomplish it. The tricky part is determining which will work best. While the overall assessment might be to use all social media platforms (as in my example), when you analyze everything together, you might find that only using Facebook will work best.

For example, for my goal of gaining more customers, it makes sense that I would need to increase my followers. By increasing my followers, I can then work on converting them to customers. How do I get more followers? Based on everything we have talked about so far, I need to stop posting on my personal Facebook page and I need to create a business Facebook page. My personality is to help others, so most of my post will be geared towards educating my followers, offering them specials, and showing them examples of how my product can benefit them. Since I will be posting images often, I will also set up a business Instagram account. I am not going to have a website or do a blog at this time, so Twitter will not really benefit me much.

As you can see from my example above, my action list would consist of the following items:

- Create a business Facebook page
- Create a business Instagram page
- Create a customer group for posting specials

This list is your first action plan. Once you have completed all the things on this list, you can then develop your marketing action plan.

MARKETING ACTION PLAN

Linking Together

Create a daily marketing action plan.

NOW that you have completed all the steps in your action plan from the last chapter, you are ready to dive in and start meeting those goals. Slow down just a minute – excitement on getting your business pages complete can often lead to hasty posting. Before you start posting anything, you need to make your marketing action plan. To do this, you will need to refer back to your goal list. You have completed the broad steps to getting your marketing started, but now it is time to think about you, your personality, and how far out of your comfort zone you are willing to go.

You will now need to complete the same process you completed earlier, to create your daily marketing action plan. Go back through your goal list and look at those tasks you wrote beside each one. Take each of those tasks and make a new list you will use to complete daily actions.

The key to making this list is to think about YOU. Do not make this list, copying from a competitor or another team member. Remember, this list needs to showcase you, not someone else.

Going back to my same example of increasing my number of customers, based on my personality, my list might look like this:

- Create 1 post daily that provides education/information about my product.
- Create 1 post weekly, playing a game to engage interaction with my followers.

- Create 1 post weekly with a special for my customers.
- Create 1 post daily to post in other groups to encourage new followers.
- Create 1 live post weekly for my current customers with a special of the day.

As you can see, my list plays to my personality, yet will still provide the desired results.

The key to a good marketing action plan is to make sure you are putting enough information and posts out there to engage people, yet not too much to turn them off to your page (we will discuss this in more detail later in the this book).

Take time now to write down your marketing action plan. Do not worry about the number of times you should post, etc. We will discuss more of those do's and don'ts in the next chapter.

DO'S AND DON'TS

Use Caution

Sometimes Less is More!

AS with anything, there are certain do's and don'ts that can make or break your marketing plan, and business in general. It is important to understand these, so you can make an informed decision. There are a handful of do's and don'ts that most people do not know, until it is too late, so keep these in mind as you make your plan of action.

Images

Using images in your marketing is a smart idea. Remember, we are living in a time where visualization is king! For those of you that are in direct sales, most often your direct sale company will provide you with many images to use. While it is great these are done for you, keep in mind that every other direct sale vendor in the company will be using the same image, do you think this will make you stand out from the rest?

If you use the provided image in your post, chances are, thousands of others will see the same image. It is important for you to use unique images. You can still use the provided image as a base, but make sure you tweak it to be unique to your post. It is unique images that attract attention.

For those not in direct sales, NEVER EVER use an image you have not paid for or gotten permission to use from the owner. What you may not know, is that every image you "copy" or "borrow" online has a tracking ID attached to it. You WILL get caught using that borrowed image and the fines associated with it are extremely high – high enough to bankrupt your business. Sharing an image/post on Facebook is acceptable, but again remember that image has already been posted by hundreds or thousands of others, so if you are trying to attract interaction, new unique images will work best.

In the next chapter, we will discuss tools you can use to manipulate your company images to make your own, as well as, places you can purchase images to use that will not break the bank.

Content

You have probably heard the saying, "content is king." Content writers, good content writers, are hard to come by, rightfully so! While there are hundreds of people and companies online that claim they can write you the "best content to attract new sales," most often that is not so.

While I have written more than 12,000 pieces of content for other businesses, I always tell every person I have ever written for, make sure you tweak it to fit your personality. The best content you can post is something from you. It does not have to be perfect, but it does need to sound like you!

You have heard the phrase that people will do business with those that they know, like and trust. Posting content that comes from you, will help your followers get to know you. When you sit down to write content for a post, think about the message you want to give your readers and followers. Keep it simple and honest.

The basic rule for a post is that it should not be more than 100 words. Too much content and your readers will pass over because they do not want to read it. If you are doing an educational or informational post, keep with the 100 words, but place a link in the post to drive them to the full article. This will give them the choice to read the full article.

As with "copying or borrowing" images, the same goes with content. Do NOT copy or borrow content. I am sure you know of plagiarism, but may not know, that again it is tracked online and if caught can ruin your business.

In the next chapter, we will discuss tools you can use to help you make sure your content is original and not violating any copyright or plagiarism laws.

Posting

There are a lot of differing opinions on how much social media posting you should do for your business. With everything from an occasional post is good, to posting 20 times a day, and everything in between. I can tell you that it varies depending upon you and your goals.

I have done several years of testing doing social posts for various types of businesses, and the one constant is that every business is different based on a variety of points. Here are the basics of posting:

1. At the very least, you need to post on social media at least once a day to gain consistency and attract followers. Your audience is looking for consistency. If you post every day for a week and then post nothing for 3 days, you will most likely lose some of your audience. This goes to back to the know you, like you, trust you concept. Your followers want to count on the fact they will get a post from you daily (trust).
2. The "sweet spot" for number of posts per day seems to be between 2-4 posts per day. There may be occasions where you will do more (again on occasion), but good quality posts have more value than just posting anything. Planning your posts, a week in advance will give you a well-rounded week of posts, and keep your audience engaged.
3. Your posts need to cover a variety of things – games, did-you-know, specials, educational, fun, etc. Mix up your posts each day, and NEVER use the same post in multiple places. For example, if you are trying to get followers on your page and want to post in different groups to attract new followers, make sure the post is different in each group.
4. Scheduling your posts is probably just as important as writing or creating your post. Luckily, there are many tools you can use to help with scheduling your posts and finding the best times to get your message out there.

One of the most common misconceptions regarding posting is, "the more I post, the more traffic I will get on my page." More traffic means more followers, means more sales. This could not be further from the truth. Just because you post 10 times a day, does not mean that what you are posting is quality info. Posting the same things day after day will only turn your audience away and eventually have them unfollow you and possibly even block you. Your success on posting on social media means you must give your audience what they are looking for – variety!

Think about this – if you consistently post (or re-post) sales pictures from your company with no other interaction, your audience will get the feeling that you are not invested. You cannot even take the time to create a unique post for your audience! The feeling they will have is that you are only looking to get a sale out of them. Where is the know you, like you, trust you in these posts?

Personal

The biggest and number one mistake you can make on your business social media pages, is post anything personal. This is why you have separate pages for your personal and business posts. DO NOT post personal things on your business page. You need to keep your business page professional at ALL times.

You do not need to explain to your customers why you were not available, just post that you will not be available for orders during a specific time. You do not need to explain to your audience you had the worst day (week, or month) of your life. If you have customers that are friends, they will like your personal page and can get all the details of your personal life there.

Keep it professional!

Boosting

Boosting a post may seem like the right thing to do, in order to gain more exposure, however, you may be boosting the wrong post. Too many people I have worked with have spent hundreds, even thousands of dollars boosting posts on social media, trying to get more exposure, more followers, more customers, more sales.

Yes, boosting posts has its benefits and its place. You MUST choose the right post to spend advertising dollars on. You have heard me mention in the beginning of the book, that organic followers, organic customers are the best. Gaining organic followers, organic customers, and organic sales, is based on people finding you for specific reasons – a post you did resonated with them, a product you posted they have been looking for, or someone referred them to you (the best kind of traffic). An organic audience will typically stay with you, will interact with you, will purchase from you. These are the type of people you want!

When you do a boost to gain traffic, you must choose the appropriate post. It needs to be engaging and it must fill one of the needs I just mentioned. If it does not, yes you will get likes and followers, but they will be just a number. They will never engage, never buy, just a number.

Be smart with your marketing and advertising dollars!

TOOLS TO HELP YOU MASTER SOCIAL MEDIA

Work Smarter Not Harder

Master social media without spending hours every day in front of the computer.

S INCE so many small business owners, especially home-based business, have full-time jobs, and families to take care of, and life... it is important to find ways that you can still market on social media without spending hours every day in front of your computer or on your smart device. Luckily, there are many ways you can work smarter and not harder!

Now, I should mention here, that even though there are lots of ways you can automate some of your posts, you still need to be present on your social media. What I mean by that is, just because you can schedule all your posts for the week, does not mean you can then ignore your social media platforms all week. You still need to be available to answer questions, interact with posts, take orders, etc.

The goal is to spend time weekly planning your posts. Schedule those posts, to free you up to do other things – business and personal! Here are a few tools that I personally have used that work wonders in helping you post in advance, as well as, help you stay organized and give you analytic data to use in reviewing your action plan.

Images

If you plan on using lots of images with your posts, as we discussed earlier, you will need to purchase your images. I personally get my images in 1 of 2 places – from a local photographer that I trust, or from the website Dreamstime. While there are lots of websites available out there that have images you can purchase, I feel that Dreamstime has the best images and the most reasonable price. You can find them online at dreamstime.com

The best way to keep your images organized is to keep a folder on your desktop labeled images. Every image that you purchase, you can place in this folder. When purchasing images, you will want to get the image that is at least 300dpi and is 800x500 (on Dreamstime this is the S image). For ease of use, I would recommend renaming the image once you download it, with a name you will identify with quickly.

Depending on how you will use the image, will determine if you will need to modify the image in any way. For example, if you will use the image for a cover photo, you may want to put your business name on the photo so that shows in your cover photo. If you are using for a post, you may need to add your website url for ordering, etc.

There are several programs you can use to manipulate an image. For basic modifications you can use the program, Paint. This is loaded on most computers free. This program will allow you to resize the image, add text, highlight, etc. If you need more detailed modifications, Photoshop is a great program. This is the program I prefer and use daily.

Content

As we discussed earlier in this book, it is important that any content you use in your posts is original. I always write out my posts, using Microsoft Word or Notepad, and then check the post for copyright or plagiarism using the website CopyScape. On a side note, by writing your post in Microsoft Word, it will spell check for you, so you can copy and paste when you schedule the post free of errors.

Copyscape is the best way to check your content before posting. It is extremely cost effective and will keep you legal with your posted content. Simply copy your post into the box on Copyscape and it will return a percentage value of originality. You need to strive for 100%.

You can find this site at copyscape.com

Posting

Finding ways to speed up posting is the most sought after shortcut. No one has hours every day to sit in front of their computer and post, post, post. And, as you are aware, there are literally dozens of programs available to help you accomplish this.

Out of all these programs, I have tested and used repeatedly, to find the ones that work the best. The choice is yours, but here are my recommendations:

- Facebook has improved their scheduling of posts a great deal. So much so, that I typically use their scheduling for virtually all my FB posts today. You now can schedule posts on your main business FB page, in your groups, and even on your event pages. The only drawback to using the scheduler within Facebook, is that if you have your Instagram account tied to your business FB page, you will not be able to share the post to Instagram when you schedule.
- There are many different scheduling programs, such as HootSuite and Later, but my favorite is CoSchedule. If you have a website or blog, this is absolutely the best program to use to post your content and schedule social media posts around that article. It is easy to use and allows you to post all your social media posts directly from this one program. And, even better, it gives you analytical information about the posts. You can find this site at coschedule.com (the individual plan that starts at $20 per month is perfect for a small, individual business).

Now that we have covered using social media for your business, creating your action plan, and how to master social media with a variety of tools, now it is time to look at the 3 most often used social media platforms or channels, and some specifics you should keep in mind with setting up your business accounts and using them.

FACEBOOK SPECIFICS

Business Page, Groups, Events, & More

Bringing it all together

AS we have discussed, Facebook is the most widely used social media platform for small businesses today. Rightly so for a variety of reasons – large audience, ability to target your ideal audience, ease of use, and so much more. While Facebook is extremely popular, many still do not know of, or understand, the proper way to set up a business FB account. This chapter is to give you the broad strokes of setting up your business FB page, and how to use some relevant pieces and parts for your marketing!

There are tons of tutorials available on setting up your business FB page, including some great informational guidelines from FB. The information I am giving you here are little tidbits that I have learned along the way that might save you some time and money. . .

Business Page Settings

If you have not set up your business FB page yet, the following steps will be a good start for you. If you already have a business page, then it would not hurt to double check these settings –

- To create a business page, log into your personal account. Once logged in, click on the down arrow on the top far right-hand corner. You will see Create Page or Manage Pages. Click on that and follow the step-by-step instructions to complete your business page.

- It is important to note that you need to have fantastic images on your cover. The large banner should be changed at least every couple of months. Before moving on, include images!
- Once your page is created, click on the settings link on your business page, top right corner. There are some settings that I have found to work better than others:
    - General settings – under the heading Visitor Posts, it is best to have a checkmark in the Review Posts by other people statement – this will allow you to make sure what is being posted to your page is appropriate. Under the heading Country Restrictions, I have found changing this to only allow people in the United States to see will save you a ton of spam.
    - Page Info settings – on this tab, you will want to make sure everything is complete. If something does not apply to you, then make sure to choose the appropriate setting.
    - Templates and Tabs settings – this is where you will choose the appropriate template for your page. Most will choose either shopping (if you want to include a shop on your page) or business. Once you choose the right template for you, then you can adjust the tabs below to fit your action plan.
    - Instagram settings – this is where you will hook your Instagram account to your FB account (helps speed up posting).
- Directly under your profile picture, you will see create a username. This is your @business name that is a great shortcut to finding your business FB page. Make sure you create this right away. You can also print this on your business cards, marketing materials ect.

Once you have finalized your settings, you can then go back to the main page. Before you start to share with others and invite people to like your new page, make sure to click on your About tab and fill everything in accordingly. The most important piece here is to have your website listed correctly and make sure to tell your story. Lots of people that will view your page, will read your story! This is your chance to help them get to know you, like you, and trust you!

Groups

One of the best features of a business FB page, is that you can set up multiple groups. Instead of posting "everything" on your main business page, you can separate certain posts that would pertain to a particular group of people.

For example, you can have a group called VIP's, which all your customers who have purchased from you would go in, a Beginner group, which anyone that has not purchased or has never done your craft would go in, or even a group for just your team members to go in.

The purpose of the group is to clean up your posting on your main page. Instead of posting sale after sale on your main page, you would post those in your VIP group, leaving sale posts on your main page as an occasional post. When you are planning your posts for the week, keep in mind that most of your posts will be done to a group, instead of your main page. And, sharing your group posts to your main page – NO – it is not needed!

My rule of thumb is to schedule my posts in the group's first, then schedule the main page posts.

You can set up as many groups as you want and may even have followers that are in multiple groups. The nice thing about having a group, is you have control over what can and cannot be done in it! Once you have set up your group, you will want to edit your group settings. Make sure all settings are completed and pay special attention to the Membership Requests sections. I have found that allowing only admins to approve memberships will save you a lot of headache and unwanted guests in your group. I always change my settings to allow only an admin of my page to approve requests and change the post approval so I must approve it to appear on the page.

Note – if you will be doing lives or online selling – you MUST have a group to do these in. More later regarding Lives.

Events

Building your brand means getting your name out there. Another cool feature on the Business FB page is regarding events. Whenever you are hosting an event, you should create an event through your business page. (Caution about creating events that you are participating in).

By using events on your business FB page, anyone that views the event, will also be given a link to your business page, and they will be able to see your event history. This can be important when you are trying to build your brand and gain followers.

Use the event feature for events you are hosting, such as classes, information meetings, demonstrations, etc. If you are participating in an event, you should NOT create an event on your business page for it. This will take away from the original event created by the host and will confuse guests. If you are a co-host of the event, ask the original host to add you as a co-host. This way, the event will show on your page under events. If you are not a host, then ask permission of the original host to do a post on the event. Include the link to your page, so those looking at the event will be able to visit your page. (Using your @link works best, such as @thecantonmarketplace).

Again, when setting up an event, make sure you complete all information accordingly. Once the event is set up, invite your followers, friends, family, etc. to attend. Keep in mind when you create an event, it will post to your main page – NO need to share to your page.

Now, that is not to say that as part of your marketing plan, you should not share the event on your page. Periodically, you should share the event to your main page with a little short snippet about it in the post area.

Posting

As we have discussed prior, posting should happen according to the action plan you created. Facebook has improved their posting features over the last few years, and there are lots of ways you can save time.

First, lets talk about how, when, where you should post.

How – whether you use an external program to help you with your posting, or use the features included in FB, make sure you follow your action plan when posting. I have found that writing out all of my posts for the week in advance helps not only my planning for the week, but I can make sure that my main page and all my groups have plenty of quality posts.

When – again, your action plan will determine when you post. Once a day, three times a day, etc. I have found it takes a good 30-60 days to look at analytical data on your posts and determine the best times of day, the best types of posts, etc.

Where – this is the hardest piece of posting for most to grasp. This goes back to the less is more concept. Doing every post on your main page and then sharing to 10 groups is NOT the way to gain organic followers or even get sales. Your best option is to post announcements, occasional sales, contest announcements, winner announcements, and informational posts to your main page. For the most part, your sales posts will go in your VIP or customer groups, including contests, specials, etc.

Instructional and demonstration posts would go in your customer or beginner groups. If you want to post something in a group that does not belong to you, make sure the post is unique. If you are trying to sell something, make sure the post is different than what you have posted in your group.

As mentioned earlier, you must be vigilant in what goes on through your page. Keep an eye on your page all day. When someone posts a response, make sure you comment, like, and interact.

Sharing

Sharing is a great concept on Facebook, but too many people abuse this feature. Going back to what we talked about before, people on FB are in multiple groups, view multiple pages, etc. Every time you share the same post to 10 groups/page, you are turning potential customers off to you and your page because of over-posting.

The sharing feature is for your customers, followers, and potential customers to use to share your posts. Engaging posts will have your followers sharing on their feeds, which leads to more organic traffic.

While it is ok to share a post you did, occasionally, it should not be the norm.

Lives

Doing lives on FB is a great way to get attention and gain new followers, however, take caution. Lives on your main page should only be quick hello type posts. If you are at an event, want to do a shout out, or create some buzz about something coming soon, those are great for your main page.

Your lives where you are selling items, doing instruction or demonstrations, etc. should always be done in one of your groups. Again, you can allow others to share your live, but you should not share your lives. The goal is to get people to join your group where they will get all your posts all the time!

Getting Likes / Followers

As you can see from the information above, many of the things you do on FB will help you gain likes and new followers. The number one thing I can tell you, is you have to do the work to get them!

I typically spend 2-3 times a day reviewing all likes, shares, etc. on my posts. Go through your notifications one at a time and as you review, invite that person to like your page if they have not done so already. This is the best way to increase your organic traffic, likes, and followers.

INSTAGRAM SPECIFICS

Tie to Facebook

Bringing it all together

AS discussed, Instagram has increased in popularity, especially since now it can be tied to your business FB page. People are visual creatures, which is why Instagram is increasing in popularity so quickly.

When you set up your business FB page, make sure that you link your Instagram page to it. This will allow you to create posts that can be shared to both your page and Instagram. If you want to do additional posts on Instagram, you will need to download the app on your mobile device.

Just as was mentioned above in the Facebook specifics, make sure you are posting relevant images and info, they are unique, and that you respond to all comments and likes. Gaining likes and followers on Instagram may seem easier, but the key is to get them to convert to following you and purchasing from you!

Be sure to log into your Instagram account and completely set up your profile. This is viewed often on this platform. The description field is small, so you may need to get creative to get it to fit, but make sure to leave enough room to add your website and/or FB link.

The two most popular posts on Instagram are, posting your item for sale, but let them request purchase information via a comment, and inspirational images are the most popular and will gain traffic.

TWITTER SPECIFICS

Perfect for Bloggers

Bringing it all together

A S mentioned earlier, Twitter is a great tool for those that have a blog or website and want to post small snippets of content. Twitter has dwindled in users but can be relevant if you are trying to educate or get information out to the masses.

While you can post directly through Twitter online or the app, it is best to use a third-party program to help you manage your posts. This will save you a ton of time and give you important analytical information. The ability to tie your blog or website to the third-party app is a huge time-saver!

Remember, if you use Twitter, you will need to interact and make sure to comment, etc. Lots of people will re-tweet engaging posts, and you will want to make sure that you thank them, comment, and follow them.

Twitter can sometimes be useful for posting a sale and gain attention, but if that is all you will use it for, you are best to skip using Twitter. Remember the key to gaining organic traffic is consistency and you should not post sale info every day!

SUMMARY

Becoming a Social Media Master

It takes consistent work!

Hope that you were able to pull some info from this book to help you become the social media master of your business. Keep in mind that most of the information contained here is from years of research and trial and error in my own business (and those that have entrusted me with their social media marketing).

Contrary to what you hear or read, social media marketing takes lots of work and does not happen overnight. The false claim that, "if I put it out there, they will come" may have been true years ago, but with so much information out there today, that is no longer the case.

You must find a way to separate yourself from all the hundreds or thousands of others marketing the same thing you are. What is the one thing that is different? YOU. You are the difference maker in your business. While the basic concepts are the same for everyone, it is you that needs to make your mark. Make your posts your own! If you are crazy in your business and that is what sets you apart – then own it! Market it! If you are known as an educator or helper – then educate and provide the support that people have come to know you for!

The one thing I can give you is never stop learning, tweaking, and perfecting yourself and your business.

DISCLAIMERS

The information provided in this book will educate you and give you the tools necessary to make informed decisions about your social media marketing. It is not intended to be a substitute for professional advice. Social Media marketing and the use of all social media platforms is complex and not covered entirely in this book. The information contained is meant to give you the broad strokes to begin yourself, and hopefully learn along the way what works best for you and your business.

INSPIRATION

Hi - I'm Tammy. . .

Born and raised in Maine, I am no stranger to hard work, or living life to its fullest. In fact, it is what drives my passion. I am the proud mom of two incredible men, who have helped me learn some very valuable lessons along the way.

While I began dabbling as an entrepreneur when I was only 11 years old, it was not until 2011 that I really found my passion for helping others. I have been an entrepreneur all my life, but 2011 is when I discovered my calling - helping others live the life they dreamed of.

I have experienced firsthand how difficult it can be to live the life you want -

After tons of research, reading, and education, I have the tools and passion to help others live the life they want, free of denial and guilt! It is now my passion to show the possibilities to others, through guidance and leadership.

I am living proof that it is possible, no matter what obstacles are in your way, to live the life you dream of - so dream big! I salute you for embarking on your journey, and I look forward to hearing your story and success!

You can attend one of Tammy's classes through her company, The Canton Marketplace, or join her Social Media Master group!

www.thecantonmarketplace.com
Facebook – @thecantonmarketplace

www.ingramcontent.com/pod-product-compliance
Lightning Source LLC
Chambersburg PA
CBHW030546220526
45463CB00007B/2998